GOD WILLING

GOD WILLING

An easier-to-read and abridged version of the classic
"Divine Conduct or The Mystery of Providence"
by John Flavel,
first published in 1677

Prepared by Hervey Mockford

General Editor – J. K. Davies

© GRACE PUBLICATIONS TRUST
139 Grosvenor Avenue,
LONDON, N5 2NH

1981

ISBN 0 9505476 6 2

The full version of "Mystery of Providence" by
John Flavel is published by the Banner of Truth Trust,
3 Murrayfield Road, Edinburgh EH12 6EL.

Set, printed and bound in Great Britain
by Billing and Sons Limited,
Guildford, London, Oxford, Worcester

CONTENTS

INTRODUCTION

"I will cry to God most high; to God who does
everything for me"
Psalm 57:2

There are two ways in which God shows himself to me
– by his word and by his works. The great glory of the
works of God in creation and providence is that they
confirm what he has said in his written word.

There is great delight in observing providence for
the people of God. Providence not only brings them to
heaven, but also brings much of heaven into their souls
on the way. The most wise God is providentially
steering all to the port of his own praise and his people's happiness, even though the whole world is busily
employed in managing the sails and tugging at the oars
with quite an opposite purpose. How great a pleasure it
is to see how the world brings about God's purposes by
opposing them; doing his will by resisting it; and enlar-
ging his church by scattering it.

There are some enjoyments in the Christian life
which are too great to be described. These are the
delights of the study of providence in your own
experience. Try it yourself; taste and see. You will
need no more persuasion. "I will cry to God most high;
to God who does everything for me" (Psalm 57:2).

When David prayed the prayer quoted above from
Psalm 57, he was in danger of being killed by King
Saul (I Samuel 24:1, 2). God answered David's request
to be taken safely out of trouble. God always answers
the prayers of his children. This working of God in all

parts of our lives, in small things as well as great, we call "providence". David's experience of God working for him in the past, gave him hope now and strength to cry to God in his trouble. So, in our day, Christians should think about the way God has worked for them in the past, so their faith and hope may be made stronger.

But the people of God cannot understand all that happens to them on their way to heaven. Although Peter did not know what was being done to him when Christ washed his feet, he was told that all would be made clear later (John 13:7). When we get to heaven, we will see, not only that it is a beautiful place, but, in addition, the beauty of the way by which we have come. It's like seeing the different parts of a watch. First of all, we see the separate pieces and then we see the whole watch put together, each part now working with all the other parts. How lovely it will be to see, in one view, the whole plan of providence and the right reason for every act of God. Though our present view is so poor in comparison with the view we shall have from heaven, there is still so much sweetness in it that I may call it "a little heaven".

CHAPTER ONE

God's special care of his people

As well as being head to his people in the church, Christ is also ruler of the whole world. He controls events in the world for the highest good of the church. My purpose here is not so much to deal with those who do not believe in God. I want to convince those who say that God exists that the special workings of his providence are not mere accidents. There are many people who call themselves Christians who look on things that happen in their lives as just natural events. They think of the affairs of the world and of God's saints as not being governed by providence, but by natural causes. That is to live as though there is no God! Let anyone who thinks this way consider the following questions:

1. How is it that, so many times, the people of God have been saved from danger and evil by a power greater than the power of nature, and in a way which has often been against the course of nature?

Waters overflow and drown all that they can, but the Red Sea was divided and a wall of water on each side allowed the children of Israel to pass safely through. Fire burns to the utmost of its power, but when Nebuchadnezzar, King of Babylon, threw the three godly young Jews into the fiery furnace, the intense flame had no power to hurt one hair of their heads, but at the same time it killed those who had thrown them into the fire. It is natural for wild beasts like lions, when hungry, to kill animals or men for their food, but those in the den where Daniel was put for a whole night did him no harm.

2.   How is it, if they are not ordered by a special providence, that natural causes work together in such strange ways for the benefit of the saints?

In the story of Joseph there are twelve steps of providence by which he became Prime Minister of Egypt. If only one had failed, the story would have been very different. In Esther's time, there were seven acts of providence fitting in with each other to bring about the downfall of wicked Haman and the saving of the Jews from destruction. God is able to do different things to take care of his people, just as a workman uses all sorts of tools in his work. In the same way as a workman takes a rough bit of wood and makes it into a work of art, so there is a most skilful hand that uses the tools in the workshop of providence.

3.   If the affairs of God's people are not governed by a special providence, how is it that the most clever and powerful means employed to destroy them have no effect, and the weak and feeble means employed for their safety are successful?

Such was the great power and skill used by Pharaoh in his attempt to destroy God's people Israel, that it would seem to natural reason to be impossible for them to escape. The Roman emperors, who conquered the world, employed all their power against the poor, defenceless church, but the church lived on! If half that power had been employed against any other people, it would certainly have destroyed them completely. God made good his promises: "Though I make a full end of all nations ... I will not make a full end of you"

(Jeremiah 30:11). And, "No weapon that is formed against you shall prosper" (Isaiah 54:17).

On the other hand, what weak and unlikely means were chosen for the planting of Christianity in the world. Christ did not choose men of authority in the courts of kings, but twelve ordinary men, the chief among them being fishermen. These were sent out, not together, but some to one country and some to another, and yet in how short a time the gospel spread and churches were planted by them in the different kingdoms of the world. From that time until our own day, a special providence has watched over Christians in times of danger and prevented all attempts to destroy them.

4. If all things are governed by natural causes, how is it that men are turned from the evil way along which they were going at full speed?

Paul was on his way to Damascus to put Christians to death when he was suddenly struck down by a light from heaven. He was turned from his purpose and was made an apostle of Jesus Christ (Acts 9:1–18). Later, when the Jews plotted to kill him as he was brought as a prisoner from Caesarea to Jerusalem, the governor Festus (though he did not know of the plot) decided to judge Paul at Caesarea and not at Jerusalem, so bringing their plans to nothing (Acts 25:1–4).

Augustine, a great leader of the early Christian church, was going to a certain town to teach the people there, and took a guide with him to show him the way. The guide missed the usual road, but taking a different route they arrived safely at the town. Afterwards they found they had escaped death at the hands of enemies who had lain in wait to kill Augustine on the road.

3

Who can fail to see the finger of God in these things?

5. If there is not an overruling providence ordering all things for the good of God's people, how is it that the good or evil which is done to them in this world is repaid to those who bring good or evil upon them?

When Pharaoh ordered the killing of all the sons born to the children of Israel, the midwives refused to obey his command. For this the Lord dealt well with them (Exodus 1:21). Rahab hid the spies sent into Jericho, and she was kept safe when all the people of the city were destroyed (Joshua 6:25). The Shunammite woman was kind to Elisha the prophet and provided a room for his use at all times, and God gave her the joy of having a son (II Kings 4:9–17). Publius, the chief man on the island of Melita, gave Paul a lodging after his shipwreck. The Lord speedily repaid him for that kindness and healed his sick father (Acts 28:7, 8).

In the same way, the evils done to God's people have been repaid to their enemies. As we have seen, it was Pharaoh's purpose to destroy the innocent children of the Israelites. God repaid him by killing all the firstborn of Egypt in one night (Exodus 12:29). Haman made a very high gallows for good Mordecai, and God so ordered it that Haman himself and his ten sons were hanged on it (Esther 7:10). Ahithophel plotted against David and counselled how to bring about his downfall. That very counsel rebounded on him and brought about his own ruin (II Samuel 17:23).

After the cruel Roman Emperor Maximinus had

ordered the Christian religion to be abolished completely, he was struck down with a dreadful disease, like Herod in the days of the apostles (Acts 12:23). Sometimes the repayment of evil has been very exact. When Naboth had been killed, Ahab was told: "Where the dogs licked the blood of Naboth, dogs shall lick your blood." And this was exactly what happened (I Kings 21:19 and 22:38).

So the scriptures are made good by providence. "Whoever digs a pit shall fall into it; and he who rolls a stone, it will roll back on him" (Proverbs 26:27), and "With whatever measure you measure out, it shall be measured to you again" (Matthew 7:2).

6.   If these things are merely accidental, how is it that they agree so exactly with the scriptures in all details?

Does God miraculously suspend the power of natural causes? This is no accident, but is in accordance with the word: "When you pass through the waters, I will be with you; and through the rivers, they shall not overflow you. When you walk through the fire, you shall not be burned; nor shall the flame kindle on you" (Isaiah 43:2). Do natural causes work for the good of God's people? This is in accordance with the scripture: "All things are yours ... and you are Christ's" (I Corinthians 3:22).

When providence keeps good men from falling into evil, or wicked men from doing evil, the truth and certainty of the following scriptures are made known in a very real way: "The way of man is not in himself: it is not in man who walks to direct his steps" (Jeremiah 10:23) and "A man's heart plans his way: but the Lord directs his steps" (Proverbs 16:9). When evil things men have done rebound on them, Psalm 9:16 is true: "The wicked is snared in the work of his own hands." Cyrus, head of the Persian Empire, let God's people go free because scripture said he should do so, although it was against his own interests (Isaiah 45:13). All the people in the world always fulfil the purposes of God, even when they don't want to do so.

7. If these things happen by chance, how is it that they occur exactly at the right time?

The Old Testament is full of examples of such events. Hagar is told of a well of water when she thinks she has left the boy Ishmael to die of thirst (Genesis 21:16, 19). The angel calls to Abraham and shows him another ram for the sacrifice when he is about to kill his son Isaac (Genesis 22:10–14). King Saul was told: "The Philistines have invaded the land", just as he was ready to take David and kill him (I Samuel 23:27). News of an attack from another direction caused the army of Assyria to retreat from Jerusalem, just as they were ready to advance on the city (Isaiah 37:7, 8). When Haman's plot against the Jews was ready to be put into operation, "on that night, the king could not sleep" (Esther 6:1). Many similar happenings to God's people in later years could be told as further evidence of the very exact way in which providence works for them.

8. If these things are merely accidental, how is it that they happen in accordance with the prayers of the saints, who know they have received very clear answers to the particular requests they have made (I John 5:15)?

Abraham's servant prayed for success as he went to

seek a wife for Isaac. His prayer was answered according to the exact words he had used (Genesis 24:14, 46). The children of Israel cried to the Lord when Pharaoh and the Egyptians marched after them, and the Red Sea divided in front of them (Exodus 14:10). King Asa was faced with an army numbering many thousands more than his own, and he cried to the Lord his God. He said: "Lord, it is nothing with you to help, whether with many, or with those who have no power. Help us, O Lord our God; for we rest on you, and in your name we go." God's answer was to give him a great victory (II Chronicles 14:11). Peter was put in prison and the church prayed day and night for him. See how their prayers were answered in Acts 12:1–12.

Who can say that the providences of God do not show him as a God who hears and answers prayer? "For the eyes of the Lord run to and fro throughout the whole earth, to show himself strong on behalf of those whose heart is perfect toward him" (II Chronicles 16:9).

CHAPTER TWO

How God works providentially in our lives

1. Providence at our birth

David praised the wonderful works of God when he thought of the way God had made him and knew every detail of his little body, even before he was born (Psalm 139:13–16). But the body is only the outside of the real man. God also made humans able to think and to love, and in these ways we are made in the likeness of God himself. See how well providence has worked for you in the first days of your life in this world, and has then brought you safely through many dangers into that place it was always God's purpose for you to be.

2. Providence in the time and place of our birth
(Sections 2 and 3 of Flavel are combined here)

God ordered the time and place where you were born. All countries are not equally pleasant to live in, and those who live in a land where God is truly worshipped and the good news of salvation by his Son Jesus Christ is freely made known, are specially favoured by providence.* The goodness of providence is seen if your parents were Christians. Their prayers, teaching and example encouraged you to seek the knowledge of God and eternal life. But even if your parents were not Christians, it is still a special providence when you find

---

* In this century the gospel can be heard by radio in nearly every country in the world. This is a providence of God that John Flavel could not have dreamed of!

9

the grace of God giving you a desire to know him, when everyone around had no such desire because their minds were opposed to God and his ways.

3. *Providence at our new birth*

Providence is most clearly seen in the way God turns men and women from thinking only of themselves and gives them a real knowledge of himself. This is the greatest benefit you ever received from providence and you will love to think and talk about it. Jacob's "Bethel" experience was always sweet to his thoughts (Genesis 28:10–22). Other saints have also had their "Bethels" – places where God made deep impressions on their hearts – which can never be forgotten.

The strange and wonderful way providence works in bringing people to a knowledge of God is seen in many instances in the Bible. A little girl taken captive from the land of Israel was given as a maid to the wife of Naaman, captain of the army of the king of Syria. She told her mistress of the power of God through Elisha the prophet, and Naaman was cured of his leprosy (II Kings 5:3). Christ had to go through Samaria and at noon he rested on Jacob's well. What a number of good and great providences followed from this "ordinary" happening. First the woman of Samaria, and then many more people in that city, were brought to believe in Christ (John 4:4–42). Philip joined the chariot of the Ethiopian just as that man's mind was prepared to receive the first light of the knowledge of Christ while reading the book of Isaiah (Acts 8:26–35).

Since those early days, providence has used many different ways to turn men to Jesus Christ. A page of a good book, used as a cover for something bought in a market, was the means of converting a preacher in Wales. The reading of a good book has often been the means of bringing people to Christ. Sometimes preachers have, for one reason or another, changed their subject at the last minute, and someone listening has been brought to a knowledge of themselves and of the Saviour. Keepers of prisons have been converted through the words spoken by the good men who have been imprisoned, like the jailer at Philippi in the days of Paul (Acts 16:25–31). Wicked men have gone to hear a preacher in order to mock him and make trouble, but God has met with them and shown them their sin, and they have sought and found forgiveness.

I knew of a young man who came to England on a ship from America. He had tried to take his own life and was very near the point of death. I saw him the morning after his attempted suicide and made him see how necessary it was to turn from his wrong thoughts and believe in Christ in order to have eternal life. He made a very serious request to God that these things should be worked out in his soul. I went away without hope of seeing him again, but he was still living in the evening. He said the Lord had given him help to turn from his sin, but one thing troubled him. Would Jesus Christ apply his blood to him since he had shed his own blood? I told him Christ shed his blood even for those who with wicked hands had shed the blood of Christ, and that was worse than what he had done. He then said: "I will come to Christ and let him do with me what he will." The next morning, to the great surprise of everyone, he was much better. He returned to full health. He went back to America and I had a letter from a friend saying that if ever God had done a great work, it was in the life of this young man. How strange are the ways of providence in leading men to Christ!

As providence orders very strange events when awaking souls, so the work goes on until the souls are saved completely. I remember the story of a man who had turned from his evil life and from his wicked friends. But after some time had passed, he was tempted to go back to the way of evil. Providence brought him to see his condition by bringing to his mind Proverbs 1:24–26. He was very troubled and thought his sin could not be pardoned. But God showed the scripture in Luke 17:4 and this brought a settled peace to his mind and heart. There was a good woman who felt that God had left her. She ended up in such a state of despair that she refused all comfort. One day, a Minister of the Gospel went to see her. She took a glass from the table and said: "I am as sure to be damned as this glass is to be broken." She threw the glass to the ground with all her strength, but, to the surprise of both of them, the glass didn't break! The Minister showed her that this was the work of providence and from that time her state of mind greatly improved.

And now, have you been as thankful as you ought to have been for this greatest of all favours? There are many kinds of mercies given to men by the hand of providence, but none like this. Think how providence had a purpose for your eternal good, which at the time you didn't understand. God's thoughts are not our thoughts, but as the heavens are higher than the earth, so are his ways higher than our ways, and his thoughts than our thoughts (Isaiah 55:8, 9). Zaccheus had no idea what was going to happen when he climbed into the tree to see Christ pass by. What a loving purpose

Christ had for him. Christ went into Zaccheus' house to become his guest and his Saviour (Luke 19:2–10). And little did you think about the aim of providence when you went, for one reason or another, to hear the preaching of the word of God. It brought you the message of salvation. Much that is good comes to men by the hand of providence, but there is nothing like this spiritual good. This special good which comes out of the special love of God is only given to the chosen of God (I Thessalonians 1:4, 5). Salvation is made absolutely sure. As you look backward from the time you turned to God who chose you before the world was made, so you can look forward to the time when your salvation will be complete. This spiritual good is everlasting, which will still be with you when father, mother, family, property, health and life have all gone.

4. *Providence in our daily work in this life*

Providence has an eye to your well-being in this world as well as in the world to come. To live idly is not to live honestly, as scripture plainly says in I Thessalonians 4:11, 12. It's no small mercy to have an honest and lawful job. God calls many men to work for him while they're working in their ordinary occupations. Amos and David were shepherds when God made one a prophet and the other a king (Amos 7:14, 15 and Psalm 78:70, 71). Peter and Andrew were fishermen when Christ called them to become "fishers of men" (Matthew 4:18, 19).

Some people may complain that their work is too hard for them and takes up too much of their time. My answer is that the wisdom of providence foresaw this to be the most suitable and proper employment for you in which you may serve God. If you had more ease and rest, you might have more temptations and your health might not be so good. "The sleep of a labouring man is sweet whether he eat little or much: but the abundance of the rich will not allow him to sleep" (Ecclesiastes 5:12). If you have spiritual desires, you may enjoy the presence of God even in your work, and you'll have some spare time during the day when you can pray and think about his word.

If you're a Christian, God has promised never to leave you (Hebrews 13:5). Providence has ordered that position in the world which is really best for your eternal good. We are commanded to be content with what we have, even though this may be no more than our necessary food and clothes (I Timothy 6:8).

The command to Adam in Genesis 3:19 is also for us today. We are to work with all our strength, whatever we are doing. But we must be careful not to lose touch with God in a desire to get rich. "Those who want to be rich fall into temptation and a snare" (I Timothy 6:9). God it is who gives power to get wealth (Deuteronomy 8:18). Don't take on any work which you cannot bring to God in prayer, asking him to bless (Psalm 37:4, 5). Be satisfied with the position and work in which providence has placed you. Providence is wiser than you are and has planned all things for your eternal good. You can be sure of that.

5. *Providence in our family life*

Providence has a special hand in the finding of a wife or a husband, and afterwards in the gift of children. This is seen clearly in the case of Abraham seeking a wife for Isaac (Genesis 24); in the gift of the child

14

Samuel to Hannah (I Samuel 1:20); and in the birth of John Baptist to Zacharias and Elizabeth (Luke 1:13, 14). There's a lot of providence seen in providing suitable partners for us, resulting in peaceful and happy marriages. It is especially remarkable when the way one partner lives is a means of bringing eternal spiritual good to the other. "For what do you know, O wife, whether you shall save your husband? Or what do you know, O husband, whether you shall save your wife?" (I Corinthians 7:16). When both partners are Christians, what a happy providence it was that brought them into such close relationship with each other on earth, and to an eternal hope of salvation in heaven.

Great numbers of men and women are not able to enjoy these good things. If you are given these great blessings, don't forget to thank God and to live a life of praise to him. The Lord expects praise wherever you have comfort. Death will soon break up the family; so live in such a way that the parting day will be sweet.

6. *Providential benefits for our families*

You know the promises God made to his people – "The young lions have lacked and suffered hunger; but those who seek the Lord shall not lack any good thing" (Psalm 34:10). Surely, "He has given food to those who fear him; he will always be mindful of his covenant" (Psalm 111:5). The Lord's mercies are "new every morning" (Lamentations 3:23). Jacob called him "the God who fed me all my life to this day" (Genesis 48:15).

I ask you to note the way of providence from your very first day to this, so you may see what God has been to you. Sometimes God secretly blesses a little and makes it quite enough for us and our families. It was so with Elijah (I Kings 17:8–16). Many other people in more recent times have found that God sends money or food just when it is most urgently needed. The wisdom of providence is seen in supplying our real needs and not giving us everything we want. "My God will supply all your need" (Philippians 4:19). Wise providence is also seen in the way those needs are supplied. We are not given the things we need all at once. We have to pray and believe, so that the goodness of God may be seen all the more clearly when those needs are met.

Let me ask you not to forget the care and kindness of providence, which you have experienced in so many ways. Do not distrust providence in future! This is what the children of Israel did. They said: "Behold, he struck the rock so that the waters gushed out, and the streams overflowed. Can he also give bread? Can he provide flesh for his people?" (Psalm 78:20). What unbelief, even after they had seen the power of God working for them in such wonderful ways! So be content with the position in which providence has placed you. And if troubles do come, pray to God in your time of need and he will not forget you (Isaiah 41:17 and Philippians 4:6). The birds of the air don't know where to find the next meal, but God provides for them (Matthew 6:26). Remember your relationship to Christ and his promises to you, and you'll be satisfied with what you have.

7. *Providence keeping us from evil*

Providence keeps us safe from Satan's fierce attacks on

our souls. God has promised that "with the temptation he will make a way of escape, so that you can bear it" (I Corinthians 10:13). In a world of sin, the providence of God stops evil breaking out like a great flood from our sinful natures. When the men of Sodom were full of evil desires outside Lot's house, they were struck blind by providence (Genesis 19:11). Abigail was stirred up to meet David just in time to prevent him from killing Nabal and his men (I Samuel 25:34). When the good king Jehoshaphat would have made friends with the wicked king Ahaziah, God stopped him from doing so by breaking the ships he had built (II Chronicles 20:35-37).

Think seriously for a moment. Your evil natures have hurried you on towards sin and yet providence has kept you from falling. As the apostle says: "Each one is tempted when he is drawn away ... by his own lust" (James 1:14). You found yourselves like feathers in the wind of temptation. Like the psalmist, your feet were almost gone, your steps had nearly slipped (Psalm 73:2). How sad it would have been if the Lord had not mercifully saved you from your many temptations. I tell you, you can't number the mercies you have in such acts of providence. So be thankful, and don't think your escapes from sin were by accident or due to your own watchfulness or wisdom. "Keep yourselves in the love of God" (Jude 21), and "keep your heart with all diligence" (Proverbs 4:23).

8. *Providence keeping us from sickness and danger*

There are many dangers surrounding us in this world. In II Corinthians 11:23-27 the apostle Paul tells us how many times he was near death or in danger.

Providence keeps us alive although we are often ill. The eye is a small part of the body, but there are many diseases that might attack it. The Creator has, however, given it various natural coverings, including the eyelid, to keep it safe. David prays: "Keep me as the apple of the eye" (Psalm 17:8).

Many people have seen wonderful works of providence when they have gone to sea. The psalmist spoke of them in Psalm 107:23–30. Those who have spent many years at sea have been in great danger and near to eternity all their days. They have cause to praise the Lord for his goodness and for his wonderful works to men!

History gives countless examples of lives being preserved by the mercy of God, and I think most of us could tell of such providences from our own experience. Consider what you owe to providence for your protection right up to this day. Think how all the parts of your body have been lovingly kept from harm, even when they were used for sinful purposes before you knew the Lord as your God. How great his mercy and patience have been towards you!

Why has providence shown this tender care for you? In order that you should use your bodies in God's service. If you are a Christian, your body is a part of Christ's purchase; it is in the care of angels and will share in the glory and happiness of the world to come (I Corinthians 6:20; Hebrews 1:14; Philippians 3:21). How reasonable it is, therefore, that our bodies should be used, and even cheerfully worn out, in the service of God!

9. *Providence helps us to become more holy*

The people of God are told that they should be "dead to sin, but alive to God in Christ Jesus" (Romans 6:11). The Holy Spirit, who lives in us, gives us the desire to destroy sin in our bodies, and helps us to do so. The most wise God orders providence to work with the Spirit to bring about the same effect.

Paul complains sadly of the "law of sin which is in my members" (Romans 7:23) and every believer daily finds this is so, to his great sorrow. But the Spirit in the believer resists sinful tendencies from inside, and providence blocks our way on the outside, to keep us from sin (Hosea 2:6 and II Corinthians 12:7). God often lets us get into trouble, such as illness of some sort, in order that we might see and feel the strength of the sin inside us and be brought back to him. The psalmist said: "Before I was afflicted I went astray, but now I have kept your word" (Psalm 119:67). Sometimes the love God's people is set on the good things in the world. The heart of Hezekiah was set on his treasures and, after proudly showing them to men from Babylon, he was told by the prophet Isaiah that they would all soon be carried away to Babylon (Isaiah 39). Good king David loved his good-looking but foolish son Absalom with a love that was too great. God used Absalom's sudden and cruel death to make David see how wrong he had been (II Samuel 15–19).

The sin which remains in us shows itself as pride. When we are honoured, the pride of the heart grows, so that one good man has said: "He that praises me, wounds me." Our sinful hearts also give us great hopes for happiness and contentment in the things of this world. Like Job, we say: "I shall die in my nest, and I shall multiply my days like the sand" (Job 29:18). How soon such hopes come to a sudden end, by the actions of God's providence. The best of men lean on things that are given to them for their comfort, instead of leaning on God himself. So the children of Israel leaned on Egypt, but God made Egypt fail and it wounded them (Ezekiel 29:6–8). Sometimes God lets death come to a loved member of a family. In this way he turns the love of our hearts away from that person to rest in himself alone.

So, to conclude this second part, I ask you to ponder in amazement the wonder of God's dealings with us. My thoughts at this point are summed up by David in Psalm 144:3: "Lord, what is man that you take knowledge of him! Or the son of man that you think anything of him!" Solomon thought of the greatness of God and said: "The heaven and heaven of heavens cannot contain him" (II Chronicles 2:6). The prophet Isaiah declared that "the nations are like a drop in a bucket ... all nations before him are as nothing" (Isaiah 40:15 and 17). But every man is so sinful and unworthy, even in his best state. His life is an empty show and his years are as nothing in God's sight.

How wonderful that this great God should think so much about us and work for us in all his providences! He doesn't need us, but is quite happy in himself without us. We can add nothing to him. He chose us freely, by his grace and his eternal love, to be his dear people. If David could say, in Psalm 8:3, 4: "When I look at your heavens, the works of your fingers – the moon and the stars which you have established – what is man?", how much more may we say: "When we consider your Son, the only Son of your love, who is great and good beyond our furthest thoughts, Lord, what is man, that such a Christ should be put to death for him?"

Our mercies are "new every morning" (see Psalm 40:5 and Lamentations 3:23). Providence is like a fountain, from which flows out the goodness of God in things relating to this life and the life to come, in public and personal ways, in ordinary and extraordinary events, too many to number. And in all that happens to believers, the angels are looking after us (Hebrews 1:14).

CHAPTER THREE

Why we should think deeply about special providences

Having seen how God takes care of his people by special providence, we now find he has commanded us to think very seriously about his acts, especially in times of trouble. To do so will strengthen our faith (Matthew 6:28). Not to do so will displease God (Psalm 28:4, 5). If the works of providence are not properly noticed, no praise can be given to God for any of them. Psalm 107 tells of God's providential care of his people in trouble (verses 4–7); of prisoners in chains (verses 10–14); of men who are ill (verses 17–20); of sailors on stormy seas (verses 23–30); and of men in times of famine (verses 33–40). Men are called to praise God for each of these providences, and in verse 43 the psalmist says: "Whoever is wise, and will be careful to do these things, they shall understand the loving-kindness of the Lord."

By these observations our faith will be strengthened. David was encouraged by acts of providence in the past to go forward to more victories in the future. "The Lord who delivered me out of the paw of the lion and out of the paw of the bear, he will deliver me out of the hand of this Philistine" (I Samuel 17:37). Paul speaks of God "who rescued us from so great a death and is delivering us, in whom we have hope that he also will still deliver us" (II Corinthians 1:10). The disciples were rebuked by Jesus because they did not remember or understand the miracles of feeding the crowds of people with a few loaves and fish (Matthew 16:9, 10).

CHAPTER FOUR

How we should think about special providences

1. Think as deeply as you can and for as long as you can about the providences of God.

Asaph said: "I will remember the works of the Lord; surely I will remember your wonders of old. I will also think on all your work and talk of your doings" (Psalm 77:11, 12). As you remember from the beginning until now what God has been to you and has done for you, your hearts will soften before you have got half way through. If they don't, they are hard hearts indeed. There is not such a pleasant history for you to read in all the world as the history of your own lives.

Keep on looking at the way God has led you until you understand it more clearly. Elijah's servant kept looking at the sky until he saw a small cloud which soon covered the heavens. So, at first, you may look at some providences and see little or nothing in them; but look "seven times", and you will see their increasing glory, like that increasing cloud. There are so many things to be considered before you judge the value of one providence. There is the timing of an event, the personal nature of a particular happening, the way one act of mercy leads on to many others, and the unlikely means used by providence. Then we must think, above everything else, of the purpose of providence in all that happens in our lives. "And we know that all things work together for good to those who love God, to those who are the called according to his purpose" (Romans 8:28).

Finally, providence is closely related to prayer.

When God gives you the things you ask for, it's as though these providences have the signature of your prayers on them!

2.   Think how the word of God is fulfilled in providence.

Joshua could say to the children of Israel: "Not one thing has failed of all the good things which the Lord your God spoke concerning you" (Joshua 23:14). This is true for all God's people. If we're troubled about the things happening around us, see what the word of God says about such things, and we'll soon have our minds put at rest. The psalmist found this to be true when he went into the sanctuary of God. He writes: "Then I understood their end" (Psalm 73:17).

It's in our own interest to keep close to the rules of scripture. When we fail to do so, the events of providence show us where we have gone wrong, as David was shown when he had sinned so badly (II Samuel 12:11, 12). The word of God tells us that it is better to trust in the Lord than in man; indeed, scripture puts a curse on anyone who puts his trust in man instead of in the Lord (Psalm 118:8 and Jeremiah 17:5). How well God's word promises that providence will care for the godly! It says that no man will lose anything by leaving his home or possessions for the sake of the gospel (Mark 10:29, 30). The apostle Paul did just that. He described himself "as having nothing, and yet possessing all things" (II Corinthians 6:10). Many thousands, since Paul's day, have found they have been provided with more than they had before, as they obeyed and trusted the promises of God.

The word of God states that whatever condition the saints may be in, their God will never leave them, nor forsake them (Hebrews 13:5). He'll be with them even in trouble (Psalm 91:15). Ask yourself whether God has ever left you to collapse under your burdens. You may have felt like David when he said: "I shall now perish one day by the hand of Saul" (I Samuel 27:1); but like him, you've come out of trouble and God's promises have been fulfilled in every detail. You read that the word of God is the only support and relief in the dark day of sickness (Psalm 119:50, 92), and that for this purpose was it written (Romans 15:4). Isn't this truth proved by a thousand experiences? If providence has shown you such promises and assured you that the Lord loves you and will be with you, your burden is now lighter than it was before! Providence also agrees with the word which says that the only way to increase our possessions is to give cheerfully to others, as giving to God (Proverbs 11:24, 25; 19:17). The best way to enjoy inward peace of mind is to obey the written word, to commit ourselves and everything that concerns us to the Lord (Psalm 37:5–7; Proverbs 16:3).

I am not saying that believers are never afflicted. Nor do I say God always punishes every sin immediately. (If he did, who would stand? – Psalm 130:3.) But this I say; when God does afflict his children, it is a mercy. By such providences the warnings, as well as the promises, of God's words are fulfilled.

3. Be sure that you see God as the one who causes and orders all the events of providence.

God is the "Father of mercies and God of all comfort" (II Corinthians 1:3). And "Your heavenly Father knows that you have need of all these things" (Matthew 6:32). You have only to tell him what you need, to be free from anxiety (Philippians 4:6). Look at the wisdom of the free grace of God, which is the way your mercies are brought to you. They all come to you through the blood of Christ and the covenant of grace (I Corinthians 3:22, 23).

Never forget that God is sovereign. He is a Being so far greater than you, the all-powerful one who does what he pleases (Psalm 115:3). A few years ago, you did not even exist. When it pleased God to bring you into the world, you had no choice as to the place or condition into which you would be born.

God is also to be seen in sad providences. Look at the grace and goodness of God in all sad happenings. Even in the darkest moments we can see two sorts of God's goodness – mercy, in still sparing this world, and mercy, in saving his people for the world to come. So, see the wisdom of God in all your troubles! The time and amount of suffering are such that you are not left completely helpless. Look at these things and ask yourself the question God asked Jonah: "Do you do well to be angry?" (Jonah 4:9). The faithfulness of the Lord means that he will not fail to discipline when there is a need for it, nor will he forsake his people while he is doing so (I Peter 1:6 and II Corinthians 4:9). Can't you see more in God than in anyone or anything that you may have lost? He is the Rock of Ages, "the same yesterday, today and for ever" (Hebrews 13:8). It may be that two or three days have made a sad change in your circumstances; but God is what he always was; time will make no change in him. "The grass withers, the flower fades; but the word of our God shall stand forever" (Isaiah 40:8).

4. Stir up your hearts to understand the different

ways of the various providences of God
(Ecclesiastes 7:14).

There are two sorts of comforts – natural and spiritual.
There is a time when Christians should enjoy both
(Esther 9:22), and there is a time when natural comfort cannot be enjoyed (Psalm 137:2). But there is no
time when spiritual joy and comfort in God should not
be experienced (I Thessalonians 5:16 and Philippians
4:4). Even in the worst troubles that can come to a
Christian, we should ask the following questions:

   i. Why should such troubles make us forget our
      comfort in God, when they are only for a
      moment and our happiness in God is eternal?
  ii. Why should we be sad, so long as our God is
      with us in all our troubles? That one promise, "I
      will be with him in trouble" (Psalm 91:15),
      should support us under all our burdens.
 iii. Why should we who are Christian believers be
      sad, so long as we can be sure that no act of
      providence, however bad it appears, is a sign of
      God's hatred? God's heart is full of love for his
      children even if the face of providence is full of
      frowns.
  iv. Why should we be depressed when we're sure
      that, even by means of these providences, God
      will do us good? (Romans 8:28).
   v. Why shouldn't we think of our joy in God, when
      the time is so near when sorrows will vanish, and
      we'll suffer no more? "God shall wipe away all
      tears" (Revelation 7:17).

If, then, you would keep your joy and comfort in
God in all circumstances, take care not to have too

strong a love for earthly things. Think about the second coming of the Lord, and earthly things will seem very small to you. Set your heart on things that are eternal, and don't risk losing such enjoyment as your fellowship with God, for the sake of a merely earthly happiness. Whether we have more, or less, of the things of this world, let us learn to be content (Philippians 4:11, 12).

I ask those who are not Christians to consider these matters seriously. The scriptures say that hell is the eternal destiny of the ungodly. The fact that you are still alive shows God's great patience and kindness towards you. You are not entitled to any mercy, but providence lengthens your life. Doesn't the preaching of the gospel, by which you may yet escape the punishment of hell, mean anything to you? What would those who are now eternally lost say if they could be put in *your* position once more?

Turning again to the Lord's people, I ask you to consider the spiritual mercies and blessings you receive in the Lord Jesus. One of these mercies alone is enough to sweeten all your troubles in this world. "Blessed is the God and Father of our Lord Jesus Christ, who has blessed us with every spiritual blessing in the heavenlies in Christ" (Ephesians 1:3). Consider what your sin really deserves from God and what it requires to cleanse you from it. Your sin deserves eternal ruin, and yet you enjoy so many mercies! The troubles that are brought on you by providence are needed to subdue sin remaining in you. Even then, don't you find you still have a proud heart? But consider how near you are to heaven. Have a little patience and all will be as well with you as your heart can desire; "for now our salvation is nearer than when we believed" (Romans 13:11).

5. If providence delays any blessing you have waited and prayed for, do not grow weary of praying to God.

We always want things quickly. But sad providences have not yet had the desired effect on our heart. We are wrong to be impatient. The longer we wait and pray, the sweeter will be the answer when it comes. "Lo, this is our God. We have waited for him and he will save us. This is the Lord; we have waited for him. We will be glad and rejoice in his salvation" (Isaiah 25:9). The foolish child picks and eats the apple while it is green. But when the fruit is ripe it drops of its own accord and is more pleasant to eat.

Blessings are often nearest when the hopes of God's people are at their lowest. The deliverances of God's people from Egypt and from Babylon were like that (Exodus 2:23 and Ezekiel 37:11). And in our own personal concerns, perhaps blessings are delayed because we are not fit to receive them. In any case, we never do *deserve* them. Blessings are always the fruits of God's pure grace. Therefore we have good reason to wait for them with patience and a thankful heart.

6. Do not question or make judgments about ways of providence.

There are things hard to understand in the works of God as well as in the words of God. We are not to use proud earthly reasoning when we consider the works of God. Asaph tried too boldly to look into the secret ways of providence. Then he said: "When I thought deeply in order to understand this, it was too painful for me" (Psalm 73:16). Job was guilty of this also (Job 42:3). I know that there is nothing in the word or in the works of God that is opposed to sound reason, but there are some things which are above human reason. For example, human reason can see no good coming from sad events, and we are tempted to distrust providence. Take care, therefore, that you do not lean too much to your own reasoning and understanding. Nothing seems more natural than to judge things by human standards, but nothing is more dangerous!

CHAPTER FIVE

The pleasure and profit obtained from looking at what God does in providence

I must now put before you the great pleasure of walking with God and daily looking closely at his providences.

1. By this means you may enjoy close fellowship with God from day to day.

Psalm 104 is a meditation on the works of providence. The psalmist says: "My thoughts of him shall be sweet" (verse 34). Fellowship is made up of two things – God making himself known to the soul, and the soul returning answers to God. The effect on us of this fellowship is seen in four ways:

  i. As with Jacob and other saints of old, we are made to feel that we do not deserve the least of God's mercies and the truth he has shown us. We are brought to say: "I am not worthy of the least of all the mercies and of all the truth which you have shown to your servant" (Genesis 32:10).
  ii. Our love for God is enlarged by our remembering his mercies. Every man loves the mercies of God, but a saint loves the God of the mercies.
  iii. Fellowship with God, produced by meditating on his providences, makes the soul keep the keenest watch on sin against God.
  iv. It makes it easy to obey and serve the Lord. David and Jehoshaphat found that this was so (Psalm 116:12; II Chronicles 17:5, 6).

So you see what wonderful fellowship a soul may have with God, by studying his providences. O that *you* would so walk with him! When such effects as these are produced in your hearts, the Lord will say: "The favours from which you have benefited were well given!" He will rejoice to do you good, for ever.

2. A great part of the pleasure of the Christian life comes from looking at what God does in providence. "The works of the Lord are great, sought out by all those who have pleasure in them" (Psalm 111:2).

   i. See how the different parts of the character of God work together in providence. They may seem sometimes to oppose each other, but in the end, they always meet. "Mercy and truth have met together; righteousness and peace have kissed each other" (Psalm 85:10). These words refer to the return of Israel from captivity in Babylon. The truth and righteousness of God in the promise he made seventy years before seemed far away from the experience of mercy and peace which Israel now met as they came out of their captivity! The promise, so many years before, and the fulfilment seventy years later, are described as two friends who now smile and kiss each other when they meet after a long absence. Whenever the promises of God and the events which are promised meet each other, they are joyfully embraced by believing people.

   ii. You may often see your own prayers and hopes rising again as if from the dead, as you look at the works of providence. God delays the answer to our prayers and we say: "My hope from the Lord is gone" (Lamentations 3:18). But then, how full of comfort we are when these prayers are answered when we have given up all hope of receiving any response to them. The lives of Job, Jacob and David show how sometimes they had lost all hope from life, but after the strange and unexpected working of providence, they lived to see their hope and comfort restored and received "life from the dead".

iii. What great blessings providence brings to us out of those very things which we thought would bring ruin or misery. Little did Joseph think, when he was sold into Egypt, that this would be for his benefit; yet he lived to see a good purpose in it (Genesis 45:5). How many times have we been made to say, like David: "It is good for me that I have been afflicted" (Psalm 119:71). We meet our troubles at first with sighs and tears, but later we look at them with joy, blessing God for them!

iv. What an immense comfort it is for a person, who sees nothing but evil in himself, at the same time to see how highly God thinks of him. As providence watches over him, that person sees goodness and mercy following him all the days of his life (Psalm 23:6). Other men seek for good and it flies from them! But goodness and mercy follow the people of God and they cannot avoid being followed, even though sometimes they sin and go out of the right way. Certainly, God's people are his treasure and "he withdraws not his eyes from the righteous" (Job 36:7).

v. What can give such joy and comfort in all this

world like the knowledge that everything that happens to us helps us on our way to heaven? However much the winds and tides of providence seem at times to be against us, nothing is more certain than that they are bringing us nearer to God and making us fit for glory.

3. Studying what God does in providence will correct the natural unbelief in your hearts.

There is a natural ungodliness in the best hearts, and this is strengthened when we think wrongly about the works of providence. We are tempted to say, like Asaph: "Behold, these are the ungodly, who are at ease in the world; they increase in riches" (Psalm 73:12). But if we carefully observe the way God punishes wicked men, some of them in this world, and all of them in the world to come, our faith will be fully confirmed. Those providences which show the wisdom, power, love and faithfulness of God in keeping and delivering his people in all their dangers, fears and difficulties, are very clear! The Lord shows himself to his people in these things (Psalm 94:1). Think of your own experiences and ask yourself who it was that supplied all you needed in hard times. It was the Lord, wasn't it? "He has given food to those who fear him; he will always be mindful of his covenant" (Psalm 111:5). How is it that you have lived through so many dangers, sicknesses and accidents? There's no doubt but that God was in these things, and by his care alone you've been preserved. The hand of God is also plainly seen in the answers to your prayers. "I sought the Lord, and he heard me and delivered me from all my fears. This poor man cried, and the Lord heard and saved him out of all his troubles" (Psalm 34:4,6).

Haven't you also discovered the Lord's hand guiding and directing your paths, so that blessings you had never thought of have been brought to you? His people are very dear to God. He does all things for them (Psalm 57:2).

4. Keeping a record of what providence has done, will be a real support to faith in future difficult times.

It's much easier for faith to travel in a path that is well known, than to beat out a new one, where it cannot see a step in front of it. The act of faith when we first trusted in Christ was the most difficult. All later acts of faith are made easier by our first experiences. When we come into a time of fresh trouble, it's a great help to be able to say: "This is not the first time I've been in these depths, and I came out before." When the disciples had no bread, Christ had to remind them of the miracles he had done before (Matthew 16:8–11). He called them men of "little faith" because they should have trusted God, after seeing so much of his power in the past. There are two ways in which we show our unbelief – we doubt the power of God, and we doubt his willingness to help. The children of Israel thought that some things were impossible for God to do. "Can God set a table in the wilderness? Can he also give bread? Can he provide flesh for his people?" (Psalm 78:19, 20). Because we do not see the way relief can come, we think none can be expected. But all these reasonings of unbelief are overcome if we think of our earlier experiences. God *has* helped, therefore he *can* help. He has as much power and ability as he always had!

Unbelief also questions whether God will *now* be

gracious, though he has been in the past. David, and Paul, reasoned from what God *had* done to what he would do *now* (I Samuel 17:36; II Corinthians 1:10). What question can there be, after such frequent proofs of God's goodness in the past?

Unbelief may say, how can such a sinful and evil creature as I, expect that God should do this or that for me? You may reply, the mercy of God appeared first to me when I was worse than I am now, and therefore I will still expect his goodness to me to continue, though I do not deserve it. "For if while we were enemies we were reconciled to God through the death of his Son, much more having been reconciled now – we shall be saved by his life" (Romans 5:10).

5. Remembering past providences will be a continual source of praise and thanksgiving, which is the employment of the angels in heaven, and the most enjoyable part of our lives on earth.

It is said of the Lord's people of old: "They hurried to forget his works" (Psalm 106:13). Though providence fed them in a remarkable way in the wilderness, they did not give God the praise he expected (Numbers 11:6). But David stirred up all his powers to thank and bless God for all his mercies to him. "Bless the Lord, O my soul; and all that is within me, bless his holy name" (Psalm 103:1). It is not so much the blessings that providence gives us, but the goodness and kindness of God in giving them, that occupies a grateful person in praise. As David says: "Because your loving-kindness is better than life, my lips shall praise you" (Psalm 63:3). To give life, and to preserve it, are precious acts of providence; but the grace that causes God to do all this is far better than the acts themselves. We have mercies every day, and they are a great reason for thankfulness. "Blessed be the Lord, who daily loads us with goodness" (Psalm 68:19). The tenderness of God's mercy is shown in his providence. "As a father pities his children, so the Lord pities those who fear him" (Psalm 103:13). His deep feelings, as he comforts his people, are like those of a mother for her baby (Isaiah 49:15). So, to lie at his feet in holy wonder at the gracious way he stoops down to our low level in his dealings with us, is a most enjoyable thing.

6.   The careful observation of providence will make Jesus Christ more and more precious to your souls.

Through Christ, God's mercies flow to us, and all praise returns to God from us. All things are ours, because we are his (I Corinthians 3:21–23).

i.   All the blessings we have in this life, as well as all spiritual and eternal mercies, have been bought for us by the blood of Christ. By his death, Christ restores to us everything sin has robbed us of. "With Christ" God freely gives us all things; salvation itself, and all things necessary to bring us there (Romans 8:32). Whatever good we receive from the hand of providence, we must say, comes by the death of Christ.

ii.   Because we are united with Christ, everything we receive from providence is made a blessing to us. When we are in Christ, we have more than we lost through the fall of Adam.

iii. Angels are employed in the kingdom of providence, but it is Christ who gives them their orders. Whoever is the means of doing you any good, the Lord Jesus Christ gives the command for it to be done. The care of Christ for the Christians in Damascus stopped Saul from destroying them (Acts 9).

iv. As Christ opened the door of mercy by dying for our sins, so he keeps that door open by being in the presence of God for us for ever (Revelation 5:6; Hebrews 9:24). If this were not true, every sin we commit would put an end to the mercies we have. But, "if anyone should sin, we have an advocate with the Father, Jesus Christ the righteous; and he is the propitiation for our sins" (I John 2:1, 2).

v. The answers to all your prayers are obtained for you by Jesus Christ. His name makes it impossible for the Father to deny anything you ask according to his will (John 15:16). See how much you owe to your dear Lord Jesus Christ for this great and glorious privilege!

vi. The covenant of grace secures all the blessings you enjoy, even your daily bread (Psalm 111:5), as well as all other spiritual mercies. This covenant is the new testament (agreement) paid for by his blood (I Corinthians 11:25). So you must thank the Lord Jesus Christ for every good thing you receive from that covenant.

7. The careful consideration of providence has a wonderful power to make the heart full of thankfulness.

Didn't the Lord guide you by his providence when you were only a child, and didn't he keep you from the sins and miseries that many run into when left to themselves? Won't you, then, from now on, say: "My father, you are the guide of my youth?" (Jeremiah 3:4). Then, think of the changes in our lives that have been ordered for us. How much better they are than if we had tried to arrange them for ourselves. God's thoughts have not been our thoughts, nor his ways our ways (Isaiah 55:8). Our own ideas have had to make way for better things with which providence has surprised us. When it was necessary, a friend was stirred up to help you, or a place opened to receive you. Then when providence takes them away, either your need of them ceases, or some other way is opened. Think of the unparalleled tenderness of God to his people! Compare the dealings of providence with you and with others, some perhaps from your own family who may not be Christians, and wonder at the grace, the amazing grace, which made the difference. "Was not Esau Jacob's brother?" (Malachi 1:2). Think of the way providence has dealt with you and compare this with the way you have behaved towards the Lord. You have done many wrong things in the past, and yet not once can you remember having received anything but good from the hand of God. Lastly, compare your dangers and your fears with the way providence has brought you out of all your troubles. There have been dark clouds over you when your life, your freedom, or someone dear to you, has been in danger. You turned to the Lord in your trouble, and he made a way to escape, and delivered you from all your fears (Psalm 34:4).

Do not live your life in such a hurry that you have no time to sit and think of these things. Consider in your heart these wonderful discoveries of God in his providences.

8. The careful observation of providence will bring an inward peace to your minds.

The psalmist says: "I will lie down both in peace and in sleep. For you alone, O Lord, will make me live in safety" (Psalm 4:8). He is determined that sinful fears will not rob him of his inward quiet. He will commit all his concerns into God's faithful fatherly hand which has done everything for him until that moment, and he doesn't mean to lose the comfort of one night's rest. Two things can destroy the peace of our lives – thinking too much about past disappointments, or fearing them in the future. As we think about providence there are a number of things that naturally and helpfully bring peace to the mind of a Christian, even while events around him are uncertain. For example:

   i. The supreme power of providence over all things. This is seen in Jacob's life. He said to Joseph: "I had not thought I would see your face, and, lo, God has showed me also your seed" (Genesis 48:11). Nothing is outside the power of God in providence.

  ii. The deep wisdom of providence. How often we have been looking for good to come from something that appeared beautiful, and have turned away from the face of something that appeared threatening. Yet, in the end, providence has shown us that the danger was in what looked beautiful, and the good was in what we had feared!

 iii. The past working of providence for us. "The Lord has helped us until now" (I Samuel 7:12). He is the same God now as he was in the past, and his faithfulness does not fail.

iv. When the Christian grows careless in his spiritual life, it is usually God's way to prepare something to discipline him, until his heart is made humble and more holy. Then the Lord changes the voice of his providence and says: "Return, you backsliding Israel ... I will not cause my anger to fall on you; for I am merciful, says the Lord, and I will not keep anger forever" (Jeremiah 3:12, 13).

v. Comparing the way God deals with us with the way he treats the other creatures he has made, brings us fresh hope. He takes care of the birds of the air, for whom no man provides, and the grass of the field. Can we really think he will forget his own people, who are of so much greater value? (Matthew 6:26, 30). Thinking of the care that providence has for the enemies of God in feeding, clothing and protecting them, even while they are fighting against him, must bring peace to our minds. Surely he will not fail to provide for the people on whom he has set his love, to whom he has given his Son, and for whom he has designed heaven itself.

9. The careful consideration of the ways of God in his providences towards us helps to increase holiness in our lives. "The Lord is righteous in all his ways and holy in all his works" (Psalm 145:17).

God sometimes uses wicked people to do what he has planned, but his purposes are most pure. His holiness is not affected by the sinfulness of man, any more than the sun is affected by the rubbish heap on which it shines. His providences stop us from sinning and so help to make us more holy. Too much prosperity might make us proud, so some things we may have desired are not given to us. Perhaps we have a weak or diseased body, and by this means God keeps us from the evil we might have done if we had been strong and healthy.

If we do sin, our Father is angry. He then uses providential events to bring us back to himself. The power of Christ's blood cleanses us from sin, but providence brings us to a point where we admit how wrong we have been and how right God is to discipline us. David cried: "O Lord, do not rebuke me in your wrath; and do not chasten me in your fury. For your arrows stick fast in me, and your hand presses heavily upon me" (Psalm 38:1, 2). So we are made to see, more clearly, the evil of sin, and we are warned against sinning in the future. "I have borne chastisement, I will not be wicked" (Job 34:31). What happy providences they are that make the person for ever afraid of sin! Whether such events bring us comfort or pain, they increase our holiness by drawing us back into the presence of God.

10. Finally, the consideration of providence will be of the greatest use to us when we come to die.

When Jacob was dying, he spoke of the dealings of God with him in the various providences of his life (Genesis 48:3,7,15,16). So did Joshua (Joshua 24). Christians! The hour of death will be sweetened if you think of the different ways God has shown his care and love to you all through your life.

i. The time of death is often the time when people are attacked by Satan with terrible temptations. He tries to make them think that God does not love them or care for them. But the Christian who remembers the times all through his life when God has answered his prayers and given him what he needed, will not believe these tales of Satan. He will say: "God has had a tender fatherly care of me ever since I became his child. He never failed me yet, and I cannot believe he will do so now." "Having loved his own which were in the world, he loved them to the end" (John 13:1). "For this God is our God forever and ever; he will be our guide even to death" (Psalm 48:14).

ii. At death, saints commit themselves into the hands of God and enter into that new state which, in a moment, will be so different. Christ sets us an example: "Father, into your hands I commit my spirit" (Luke 23:46), and Stephen, at his death, said: "Lord Jesus, receive my spirit" (Acts 7:59).

There are two very difficult acts of faith – the first act and the last. The first is a great venture, when the person throws himself on the mercy of Christ; and the last is also a great venture, when the person throws himself into the ocean of eternity on the credit of Christ's promise. But the first venture is much more difficult than the last. By the end of life, the believer has come to know Christ as a faithful friend, whose many visits have been sweet. So, with great assurance, the Christian may throw himself into the arms of God with whom he has so long talked and walked in this world!

iii. At death, the people of God receive the last mercies they will receive in this world from the hand of providence. We shall have to give an account of the way we have used all the blessings God has given us, and how can this be done unless we try to keep some record of them now?

iv. At death, we should leave to those who are left behind a good report on the way God has dealt with us in this life. As Joshua said, in his last speech to the people: "And today I am going the way of all the earth. And you know in all your hearts and in all your souls that not one thing has failed of all the good things which the Lord your God spoke concerning you. All has come true to you. Not one thing has failed" (Joshua 23:14).

v. At death, we begin a life of praise and thanksgiving, and enter the same everlasting happy employment as the angels. I don't doubt that the providences in which we were concerned in this world will be a part of the song we shall sing in heaven. So let us tune our hearts and tongues while we are here, by meditating daily on what God has been to us, and done for us.

CHAPTER SIX

The consequences of the previous chapters

1.   It is your duty to believe that God is in all that happens to you. If he gives comforts, it is a great evil not to see his hand in them. If he sends troubles, you should know that they do not arise out of the ground, but from the hand of God.

2.   Since God does all things for you, how great is his care for his people! His tender care is so great that he does not take his eyes off you (Job 36:7). In case anyone should hurt you, he himself will guard and keep you day and night (Isaiah 27:3). You are too dear to him to be trusted to any hand but his own. "All his saints are in your hand" (Deuteronomy 33:3).

3.   Since God does all things for you, are you not obliged to live for God? Our desire should be, as someone has said: "O that I could be to God as useful as my hands are to me." The purpose of all that God has done for you is to make you a blessing to other people. "What shall I give to the Lord for all his benefits to me?" said the psalmist (Psalm 116:12). God is always doing you good, so you should be active for him. He is acting every moment for you!

4.   Since God does all these things for his people, do not distrust him when new difficulties arise. You have often failed to trust him in the past. Don't fall into distrust again. Learn this great truth. If you trust in God and wait quietly on him to save you out of trouble, he cannot and will not fail you!

5.   Since God does all things for you, pray to him

about everything. You will certainly never have what you desire or work for, unless God works for you. Even though he may have purposed to do what you desire, he still expects you to ask him for it. Then when you have prayed, whatever you ask is really yours already.

6.   Since God does all things for you, then it should be your chief concern to please him in all things. No troubles can harm a Christian whose one desire is to please God. As a spark of fire is easily put out in the sea, so the favour of God will cause troubles to have no ill effects. Since it is God who does all things and who rejoices over us to do us only good, we are safe even in the greatest of troubles and dangers. Let us be guided by the divine wisdom of the Bible. Fear nothing but sin. Make it your chief concern to please God and to trust him in all you do. These are sure rules for your safety and blessing in all the uncertainties of this life.

CHAPTER SEVEN
(this also includes Flavel's chapter eight)

Practical problems

1. How can a Christian discover the will of God in difficult and puzzling circumstances?

We must first consider what is meant by the will of God. It is twofold. There is the secret will of God, and there is his revealed will. "The secret things belong to the Lord our God, but those things which are revealed belong to us" (Deuteronomy 29:29). We can only concern ourselves with the revealed will of God. This is made known to us either in his word, or in his works.

>   i. There is a great variety in the things revealed. The really important matters of the Christian faith are very clearly shown to us in the word, but things which are less important are sometimes more difficult to understand.
>   ii. There is a great difference in the persons to whom God reveals his will. Some are like strong men, and others like babies (I Corinthians 3:1). Some are well able to understand what they should do, and others cannot understand so easily.
>   iii. The ways God reveals his will to men are also very different. In Old Testament days God showed men what to do in a special personal way, as when Samuel chose Saul to be king (I Samuel 9:15–17), and when David asked the Lord whether he should go and fight the Philistines (I Samuel 23:2, 4). But now we have the whole of the Bible for our guide, and must

not expect special revelations. We must search the scriptures, and where there is no particular rule to guide us, we must apply the general rules of scripture to our particular problem.

We may, however, still be in doubt as to what to do. In that case, we should not look at providences by themselves, to discover the will of God. The safest way is to consider providences as they follow the commands or promises of the Bible. When you have prayed for guidance and you find providence agrees with your own conscience and the best light you can find in the Bible, you may take it as an encouragement to go on in the way indicated. But if providence seems to favour anything which would be going against a rule of scripture, you cannot go that way. If providence alone is used as the rule to guide us, then a wicked man who sins successfully could claim to be guided by God. The following rules will help you to discover God's will:

i. Have a true fear of God in your hearts, and be really afraid of offending him. "The secret of the Lord is with those who fear him; and he will show them his covenant" (Psalm 25:14).

ii. Study the Word more and the affairs of the world less. The Word is a light to your feet (Psalm 119:105). It will show you what to do and the dangers to avoid.

iii. Put what you already know into practice. "If anyone desires to practice his will, he shall know of the teaching" (John 7:17). "All those who obey him have understanding" (Psalm 111:10).

iv. Pray for light; beg the Lord to guide you and not let you fall into sin (see Ezra 8:21).

v. Then follow providence as far as it agrees with

the Bible, and no further. In the day of trouble, it is time to humble ourselves under the mighty hand of God. On the other hand, it is time to rejoice in God when he sends providences which bring us comfort. "In the day of prosperity be joyful" (Ecclesiastes 7:14). We should be wise to learn what God is teaching us at these different times, as providence points them out to us.

2.   How can a Christian be helped to wait on God while providence delays the answer to his prayers?

These are two ways of looking at such delays. From one point of view, times and seasons are in the hand of the Lord our God (Acts 1:7), but from our own point of view, we expect an answer to our prayers much sooner. Now nothing can be more certain or exact than the time God has chosen to answer prayer. If you compare Exodus 12:41 with Acts 7:17, you will see the reason why Israel's deliverance out of Egypt could not be delayed one day longer. It was because the time of the promise had now come. We are disappointed at the delays of providence and begin to doubt the faithfulness of God. But his thoughts are not our thoughts (Isaiah 55:8). "The Lord is not slow as to the promise, as some think of slowness" (II Peter 3:9). The Lord does not reckon his times of working by our arithmetic. God appoints the time, and though his answer may be delayed much longer than we think, it will not be a moment later than his appointment.

During these delays, God's people may become very discouraged. Through Isaiah, God had promised that he would have mercy on his people in captivity, but they waited from year to year and nothing happened.

"But Zion said, The Lord has forsaken me, and my Lord has forgotten me" (Isaiah 49:14). David was the same. God had made such promises to him that they were called "the sure mercies of David", and yet he thought that God had forgotten him. He said: "How long will you forget me, O Lord? Forever?" (Psalm 13:1). There are three main reasons why we lose heart in this way:

i. We give way to unbelief. We do not rely with full trust and confidence on the unquestionable word of a faithful and unchangeable God. This reason for faintness of heart is given in Psalm 27:13: "I would have fainted unless I had believed." In other words, a fainting heart is an evidence of unbelief.

ii. We look at things as they appear to our senses. It is said of Abraham that "against hope", that is, against natural probability, he "believed in hope ... giving glory to God" (Romans 4:18, 20). Our spirits are kept up by looking away from things which we see with our natural eyes, and measuring everything by another rule; that is, by the power and faithfulness of God (II Corinthians 4:16,18).

iii. Satan uses these occasions to suggest hard thoughts of God. When our spirits are low, we are more prepared to listen to Satan. He always seeks to weaken our hands and stop us waiting on God.

In view of what we have been saying, it is necessary for us to be watchful, to leave everything in God's hands and quietly wait for his salvation. To help us to do this, I would offer the following thoughts:

i. You have no real reason to have hard thoughts of God, for it is possible he did not promise the things you expect from him. You may have promised yourself certain things, such as prosperity and the continuance of those things you now enjoy. But where did God promise this? The promise that God will withhold no good thing is limited to those who "walk uprightly" (Psalm 84:11). Search your own heart and see whether you have not turned aside from God in your heart and life, so that he would be just in taking away those things you enjoy. In any case, all promises of good in this life are limited by the wisdom and will of God. Who told you to expect rest, ease and delight in this world? God has often told us that we must expect troubles in the world (John 16:33), and that we must "through many afflictions ... enter into the kingdom of God" (Acts 14:22). All that God has promised to do is to be with us in trouble, to supply our real needs, and to make everything work together for our good (Psalm 91:15; Isaiah 41:17; Romans 8:28).

ii. If, after praying to God for spiritual blessings, you have waited a long time and you have received nothing, I would ask you what sort of blessings you want. Spiritual blessings are of two sorts – those which are necessary for spiritual life to continue, and those which increase our joy and comfort. Blessings of the first sort are absolutely necessary and are therefore sure and unfailing promises. "I will make an everlasting covenant with them that I will not turn away from them, to do them good. But

I will put my fear in their hearts, that they shall not depart from me" (Jeremiah 32:40). Blessings of the second sort are given as the Lord sees it is good for us, and many of his people live for a long time without them.

iii. You should ask yourself what purpose you have in wanting these blessings. It may be that you don't receive what you ask for because you don't want the blessing for the right reason (James 4:3). Sometimes we ask to be freed from trouble merely because it destroys our pleasure in the world. In fact, the troubles are given in order that we might live a life of greater obedience.

iv. Are you really prepared for the will of God to be done? The thing that pleases you is the enjoyment of your desires, but God is pleased when you desire only to do his will. Blessing cannot come to you until you want to do the will of God with your whole heart. David had to wait a long time for what he had been promised, and in the meantime his soul was made "like a weaned child" (Psalm 131:2). If David and many others have had to wait a long time for God's blessing, why shouldn't you?

v. Will you lose anything by patiently waiting on God? Certainly not. It is much better to know the grace of God working in your life than to enjoy comfort. The Lord is giving you a lesson in faith and patience, and making you more concerned to do his will. When the desired blessing comes, it will be much more enjoyable because of the exercise of your faith and prayer.

vi. If the blessings you expect from God are not worth waiting for, it is foolish to be troubled because you do not have them. All that God expects from you is that you wait for his mercies, as a free favour. Think of the many promises made to those who wait on the Lord. "Blessed are all those who wait for him" (Isaiah 30:18); and, "Those who wait on the Lord shall renew their strength" (Isaiah 40:31).

vii. Remember how long a time God waited before you turned to him and obeyed his word. Isn't it right that God should make you wait for his blessing? Our unbelief has made him cry: "How long will it be before they believe me?" (Numbers 14:11), and, "How long will your vain thoughts lodge within you?" (Jeremiah 4:14).

viii. The fact that you have become tired of waiting is a great evil in itself. Probably you would have had your mercies sooner if your spirits were more quiet and ready to submit to his will.

3. How can a Christian know when a providence is working for his highest good, and comes from the love of God?

God can work good for his people out of the worst of evils (Romans 8:28). Sin can never do anyone any good, but God's providences can make even the event in which sin is present, bring good to his people. We cannot know from the actual things happening to us whether they are working for our good or not. Many wicked, unbelieving people "have more than heart could wish" (Psalm 73:7), so we cannot judge God's love to us by the number of natural blessings we receive. It is the way these things happen to us, and the effect they have on us, that will show us whether they are sent from the love of God and are for our spiritual good.

    a. Let us first look at those events which bring trouble and sorrow. We may know that they are really blessings from the love of God when they occur in the following circumstances:

        i. They come at the right time, either to keep us from falling into some sin, or to bring us back from a careless spirit into which we have fallen. "Since it is necessary, you are being put to grief" (I Peter 1:6).

        ii. God chooses certain troubles for us which will be most suited to our individual characters. He often takes away those particular comforts which take up too much of our time, and draw us away from the love and delight of our souls in God. He is like a doctor who exactly measures the strength of his medicine for the particular one who is sick. "In measure by measure, when sending her away, you punished her. He takes away by his rough wind, in the day of the east wind. By this therefore shall the iniquity of Jacob be purged" (Isaiah 27:8, 9).

        iii. It's a good sign when troubles turn our hearts against sin and not against God. When wicked men are in great trouble, they turn against God. "And men were scorched with great heat, so that they blasphemed the name of God – who has authority over these plagues" (Revelation 16:9). But godly men condemn themselves and give glory to God. "O Lord, righteousness belongs to you, but to

56

us the shame of our faces, as it is today" (Daniel 9:7).

iv. A sure sign that troubles are sent from the love of God is when they cleanse the heart from sin, and leave the life more pure, heavenly and humble than before. How many Christians know that this is true! After they have been brought through some great trouble, they see no beauty and find no more taste in the world than in the white of an egg. Sadly, these good effects do not last, and this is why God has to discipline his people again and again.

v. Anything that helps to increase our love to God must come from the love of God to us. If his grace is in our hearts, we shall cling closely to him when we are in great trouble. We shall behave like the psalmist: "All this has come upon us, yet we have not forgotten you ... our heart is not turned back, neither have our steps turned aside from your way ... though you have covered us with the shadow of death" (Psalm 44:17–19).

vi. We shall know that God is blessing us in our troubles when we find he is teaching us more of the evil of sin, the emptiness of this life, and the certainty of those things that cannot be shaken. "Blessed is the man whom you chasten, O Lord, to teach him out of your law" (Psalm 94:12). The Christian never sees things in a truer light than when he is under the discipline of God.

b. Secondly, let us look at those events which bring

us joy and happiness. Comfortable and happy circumstances do not always mean that God's blessing is in them. The success or prosperity which makes men forget God, or is used to arouse the desires of the flesh or the pride of the heart, cannot be a means of blessing.

But those comforts and mercies which humble the soul before God, by giving a sense of unworthiness, are undoubtedly being made a blessing. Jacob said: "I am not worthy of the least of all the mercies and of all the truth which you have shown to your servant" (Genesis 32:10). Such mercies will make us want to keep away from sin and give us a greater love to God. They will never satisfy us in themselves. If we are able to serve God more willingly because of our comforts and are more concerned about the needs of others, then it is a sure sign that God is blessing our comforts to us. Again, it is certain that if we have obtained some good thing as an answer to prayer, it has come to us from the love of God.

4. How can we keep steady and calm in spirit when providence brings so many changes into our lives?

Providence causes changes in people's lives in all parts of the world. "He gives greatness to the nations and destroys them. He spreads out the nations and leads them away" (Job 12:23). Many have been like Naomi, whose condition was so strangely changed that the people of Bethlehem said: "Is this Naomi?" (Ruth 1:19).

As great heat and cold try the health and strength of our bodies, so changes in our lives made by providence try the strength of God's grace in our hearts. Hezekiah was a good man, but his weakness was shown up when providence brought him into pain and sickness (Isaiah 38). David's spirit was not always quiet and untroubled when danger was all around him. He tells us: "In my prosperity I said, I shall never be moved ... you hid your face, and I was troubled" (Psalm 30:6, 7). Paul was truly rich in grace when he said: "I know both how to be humbled and I know how to abound. Everywhere and in all things, I have been taught how to be both full and hungry – both to have plenty and to have less than enough" (Philippians 4:12).

Let us consider further how we may be kept to a great degree in a peaceful state of heart and mind in all circumstances.

    i. When our circumstances are comfortable, always remember how changeable all things are. The things in which you glory today, may not be yours tomorrow. "For riches certainly make themselves wings; they fly away like an eagle toward the heavens" (Proverbs 23:5). Hezekiah gloried in his treasures, and the prophet had to tell him that, in a short while, none of those treasures would be left (Isaiah 39:2–7). You do not know what evil hearts you have until some providence like this makes you realise how little you love God, and how much you still love the things of the world. When you were poorer than you are now, didn't you know God better and love him more?

    ii. When everything seems to be against us; here we may go to the other extreme, and need help to keep our hearts steady. Providences which bring trouble and sorrow are of great use to the people of God. In fact, God's people cannot live spiritually without them. The best Christian soon finds a sad falling off of the life of God in his soul, if he has no troubles. But nothing can separate the people of God from Christ. "Who shall separate us from the love of Christ? Shall trouble?" (Romans 8:35). Job found this to be true (Job 19:25). The longest day of trouble has an end, and if a thousand troubles are appointed for you, they will come to an end at last. As Paul says: "The lightness of our affliction (which is but for a moment) is working out for us a far more excellent eternal weight of glory" (II Corinthians 4:17).

iii. When everything seems uncertain and we do not know which way the providence of God is working, think how useless it is to be full of care and anxiety in such a situation. "Which of you by being anxious is able to add one cubit to his height?" (Matthew 6:27). By wrong anxiety, we shall only lose our peace and lower our spirits. We cannot change anything in our circumstances. Instead, we shall avoid much trouble and pain by waiting quietly till we see how providence is bringing about the purposes of God in our lives. We may also rest our minds on the faithfulness of God. We have the divine authority of his word that he is bound to make all our concerns end in happiness. Not only our eternal salvation, but also all our interests in this life, are completely safe in his hands. Be quiet, therefore, in the certainty of the happy outcome of your present difficulties. "Roll your works on the Lord, and your thoughts shall be blessed" (Proverbs 16:3).

5. Finally, how can a Christian bring himself to accept the will of God when he sees that great trouble and sorrow are coming towards him?

However difficult it seems, we can do this through Christ who strengthens us (Philippians 4:13). But without him we can do nothing (John 15:5). He does not say: "Without me you can do but little", but, "without me you can do nothing at all". It may be that sickness in ourselves or in our family grows worse, and we are afraid it may end in death; or we may be alarmed at the possibility of war and the loss of all our comforts. We are ready to say, as the widow said to Elijah: "What do I have to do with you, O man of God? Have you come to me to call my sin to remembrance and to kill my son?" (I Kings 17:18). Satan then takes advantage of our sinful hearts and makes our thoughts more troubled by adding his own suggestions, and we cannot tell which thoughts are ours and which are his. Our soul becomes weakened, like a man who is awake all night thinking of a hard journey he has to make the next day, and when tomorrow comes he faints halfway because of lack of rest the night before!

It should be the Christian's greatest concern to accept the will of God and quietly commit the outcome of all events to him. In this way, David said to Zadok the priest: "Carry the ark of God back into the city. If I shall find favour in the eyes of the Lord, he will bring me again and show it to me, and its dwelling place also. But if he says this, I have no delight in you – behold me, and let him do to me as seems good to him" (II

Samuel 15:25, 26). This was a lovely and truly spiritual attitude to take. But the giving up of our wills to God is difficult. We'd be sure of peace if we could only bring our hearts to do this. It will help us to do this, with God's help, if we use the following suggestions:

i. Try to get a deep and firm sense of the great wisdom of God and of your own foolishness and ignorance. "His understanding cannot be told" (Psalm 147:5). His "thoughts are very deep" (Psalm 92:5). How often we have been forced to say our opinion was wrong, and we have made mistakes! We are often guided by other people who are wiser or more skilful than we are, such as doctors or lawyers. How much more should we give up our human reason and small understanding to the great, all-seeing and all-wise God. It's nothing but pride that makes it so hard for us to do this.

ii. Consider very carefully the sinfulness of bringing trouble on yourself with anxious thoughts, as though there was some doubt whether providence would do you good! These thoughts are the result of pride and unbelief, and they are useless to do us any good. We can't turn God back from his purpose, and shouldn't doubt his goodness.

iii. See what examples there are in scripture of those who gave themselves up to the will of God much more than you have done. When God called Abraham to go out from his own country into an unknown future, he obeyed at once. Paul knew that when he went to Jerusalem he was in great danger of prison and death, but he and the

62

Christians he was leaving behind were able to say: "The Lord's will be done" (Acts 21:14). Far greater still is the example of our dear Lord Jesus. When the Father gave the cup of suffering into his hands in the Garden of Gethsemane – a cup of the anger of the great and terrible God – his great sorrow made him cry out: "Abba! Father, all things are possible to you. Take away this cup from me" (Mark 14:36). Yet, submitting to his Father's will, he said: "But not as I desire, but as you will" (Mark 14:36). What is your situation compared with his?

iv. Think of the special advantages of a will that is brought into line with God's will. There's a deep contentment, a kind of Sabbath or sense of rest, in the spirit of a man who fully accepts the will of God for his life. Luther said, to someone who was greatly troubled in his spirit: "The Lord shall do all for thee, and thou shalt do nothing but be the Sabbath of Christ." It is by this means that the Lord "gives his beloved sleep" (Psalm 127:2). Though believers live in the middle of many troubles, yet with quiet minds they keep themselves in the silence of faith, as though they were asleep. The attitude of submission to God makes a man's spirit fit for communion with God, and brings blessing nearer. So regret no more, argue no more, but lie down quietly at your Father's feet, and say in all circumstances and at all times: "The will of the Lord be done."

POSTSCRIPT

Because memory so often fails, it is a good plan, as we read the scriptures, to keep written records of the ways God has acted in providence. This will help us to compare our present experiences with those of the past, and preserve their value to us for future days.

SOME OTHER
GRACE PUBLICATIONS TRUST TITLES

LIFE BY HIS DEATH

An easier-to-read and abridged version of the classic "The Death of Death in the Death of Christ", by Dr. John Owen, 1616–1683.

This is the first in the series GREAT CHRISTIAN CLASSICS in modern English. It is prepared by H. J. Appleby and the Foreword is by Dr. J. I. Packer. Owen published his original work in 1647 and it is suggested that no-one has ever succeeded in refuting the thesis that Owen here so fully expounds and defends from the Scriptures.

"To recover the old, authentic, biblical gospel, and to bring our preaching and practice back into line with it, is perhaps our most pressing present need. And it is at this point that Owen's treatise on redemption can give us help". From the Foreword by J. I. Packer.

". . . a brilliant abridgement of that wonderful book. The whole church of Christ stands in debt to John Appleby for undertaking this work. It will open the door into Owen's volume for countless believers who might otherwise miss its treasures". Stuart Olyott in Evangelical Times.

Paperback, 100 pages, £1.50.

Also, in the same series, to be published late 1981:

BIBLICAL CHRISTIANITY

An easier-to-read and abridged version of the classic "Institutes of the Christian Religion", by John Calvin.

GRACE GATEWAY BOOKS

Introductions to Great Christian Writings

1. WHO IS IN CONTROL?
An easy-to-read version of the substance of "The Sovereignty of God" by A. W. Pink, prepared by Roger Devenish.
Paperback, 60 pages, £1.20.

2. INTO LIFE
An easy-to-read version of the substance of "The Rise and Progress of Religion in the Soul" by Philip Doddridge, prepared by Roger Devenish.
Paperback, 60 pages, £1.20.

Other titles in course of preparation include:

"THE BEST THAT WE CAN BE" from William Law's "Serious Call to a Devout and Holy Life".

"WHAT'S THE GOOD OF IT?" from A. W. Pink's "Profiting from the Word".

"WHAT'S REAL?" from Gardiner Spring's "Distinguishing Traits of Christian Character".

A full list of Books, Work-books, Booklets and Tracts published by

GRACE PUBLICATIONS TRUST
(including "Grace Hymns")

may be obtained from the Secretary

Grace Publications Trust,
139 Grosvenor Avenue,
London, N5 2NH.